T0198871

Organize To Sell Your Home

Joy Rich, LL.B.

authorHOUSE®

AuthorHouse™
1663 Liberty Drive
Bloomington, IN 47403
www.authorhouse.com
Phone: 1-800-839-8640

Published by AuthorHouse   04/05/2012

ISBN: 978-1-4685-7549-1 (sc)
ISBN: 978-1-4685-7550-7 (e)

Library of Congress Control Number: 2012905930

CONTENTS

Dedicated to you; the homeowner.

May this book give you the tools you need to get your house sold.

Notes:

Chapter 1
Getting Started

As a seller, having an organized house will give you the competitive edge you need to get your house sold. An organized house will allow buyers to see the beauty and potential of your home.

Every home has good points, so you need to accentuate them. Think back to the first time you unlocked the front door and crossed the threshold into your new home. Remember the pride and joy you felt? You had fulfilled the American dream of home ownership. What a wonderful day that was. Remind yourself of all the things that made you want to buy your home. Maybe it was the location, the backyard, the size, or some other great feature. Now, all you have to do is rekindle that enthusiasm and channel it into organizing your home.

Simplicity is the key to prosperity; that can be your mantra for this project. Once your home has been simplified, it will be more appealing to potential buyers. Phenomenal results can be achieved when you organize your home with positive energy and an upbeat attitude.

How To Use This Book
You need to designate an area in your home to store your boxes once they've been packed.

You should rent a storage unit. This will allow you to get the boxes out of the house, and give it the appearance of being larger.

You would start at the beginning of the book and work your way to the end. If you have multiple bedrooms and bathrooms, just repeat the steps in each room from beginning to end when you start a new room.

Once you have decided where to start, take a picture of the room as is. The before pictures will allow you to see what you don't want the room to look like again. There's a blank page at the beginning of the chapter for before and after pictures.

Before you begin a room, make sure you have everything you need. There's a checklist at the beginning of each chapter. You will need:

1. A marker
2. A pen
3. Packaging tape
4. Scissors
5. A box for Donations
6. A box for Sale items
7. A box for Storage items
8. A garbage bag
9. A bag for recyclables
10. This book
11. Extra boxes and bags

Once a box is full, you should:

1. Tape it closed.
2. Assign it a number.
3. Write the room's name on it (for example: kitchen).
4. Write a short description of its contents on it (for example: dishes).

5. Fill out the Box List at the end of each chapter when you've completed the room. This will allow you to keep track of your boxes and the list, because the information will all be in the book! There are extra box lists at the end of the book for your convenience.

At the end of each chapter, there is a "Notes" section. You can use this for any notes you may need to make while packing, or for things you will need to do while unpacking.

Make sure to take an after picture, and place it at the beginning of the chapter below the before picture. The after pictures will set a standard for you to maintain.

Once you have finished organizing your home, you can have a yard sale and cash in on your efforts.

SNAP

This book uses the SNAP method to organizing. By using this system, you can organize any space in your home. SNAP is an acronym for:

Sort
Neaten
Assign and
Place

Organizing Ideas

In each chapter, there will be suggestions on how you can go about getting rid of items that you no longer want. There will also be various ways for you to organize the things that you do want. There are also tips on different subject matters.

Reward Yourself

There are different ways that you can reward yourself when you finish organizing a particular room in your home! This will be a nice way to celebrate your achievement.

Scent

At the end of every chapter, there will be a suggestion for ways to keep your room smelling great! This is also known as aroma therapy, which is soothing to the senses.

Maintenance

At the end of every chapter, there are ways for you to maintain an organized room. This is really helpful, because it will prevent your room from reverting back to its messy state.

Online Resource

Visit www.organizetosell.com for helpful tips and advice. You can also sign up for giveaways and contests too. This site was built with you in mind, so feel free to email your questions.

Let's get started!

Notes:

Garage: Before Picture

Garage: After Picture

Chapter 2
Garage

A garage is to a man, what the kitchen is to a woman. It deserves attention, because it makes an impact on a potential buyer. Quite often, people want a large garage to house their cars or tools, etc. However, for many people, the garage has become a dumping ground for everything; trash and treasure included. However, by sorting, neatening, assigning, and placing these items, you will have this space transformed into an oasis in no time. Once the garage is organized, it will appear larger and more attractive to a buyer.

Tip:

If you park your car in the garage, move it out before you start sorting; you'll need the space.

SNAP the Garage

Before you start, take a picture of the room. The before picture will allow you to see what you don't want the room to look like again. There's a blank page at the beginning of the chapter for before and after pictures. Before you begin organizing the garage, make sure you have everything you need. Here's a check list of everything you'll need:

1. A marker
2. A pen
3. Packaging tape
4. Scissors

5. A box for Donations
6. A box for Sale items
7. A box for Storage items
8. A garbage bag
9. A bag for recyclables
10. This book
11. Extra boxes and bags

Once a box is full, you should:

1. Tape it closed.
2. Assign it a number.
3. Write the room's name on it (for example: kitchen).
4. Write a short description of its contents on it (for example: dishes).
5. Fill out the Box List at the end of each chapter when you've completed the room. This will allow you to keep track of all your boxes in one place. As well, because the list is in the book, you won't misplace it!

At the end of each chapter, there is a "Notes" section. You can use this for any notes you may need to make while packing, or for things you will need to do while unpacking. Make sure to take an after picture, and place it at the beginning of the chapter below the before picture. The after picture will set a standard for you to maintain.

Tools
Sort
Gather all your tools together in a central location. Sort through all your tools and put all the broken or unwanted items in one pile, and everything that you want to keep in another pile.

Neaten
If the items that you no longer want are in relatively good condition, you can donate or sell them. If you have too many things that you're not going to use

within the next couple of months, you can store your extras. Place donations in the box marked "Donations". Place the things you're going to sell in the box labeled "Sale". Place the things you're going to store in the box marked "Storage." Put the things you're going to get rid of in the trash bag, and put your recyclables in another bag.

Assign

You need to group the remaining items into similar piles. You will end up with small groups of hammers, screw drivers, wrenches, etc.

Place

When finding homes for these items, use as much wall space as possible. Keep things off of the floor. You can install cupboards, shelves, or pegboard to keep your items in a convenient location. Remember to keep the items in their groups.

Screws, Nuts, and Bolts

Sort

Locate all your screws, nuts, and bolts, and start sorting them into two piles; one consisting of screws that have rusted or are defective. The other pile will consist of screws, nuts, and bolts that you want to hang on to.

Neaten

Throw out or recycle the screws, nuts, and bolts that are rusted or defective.

Assign

Divide the remaining screws, nuts, and bolts into their respective groups. You will then go through the pile of screws and continue to divide and subdivide them into smaller piles of like screws, until they are all in their corresponding heap. Do the same for the remaining piles of nuts and bolts.

Place

You can put the screws into small glass containers with lids. This will allow for transparency, which would enable you to see what kind of screws are in the containers. You can also use a screw organizer to put your screws, nuts, and bolts in.

Recreational Items and Sporting Equipment

Sort

Place your sporting goods and recreational items in a central location. Sort through them by putting the items that are broken, no longer being used, or that are no longer wanted into one pile, and the things you want in another pile.

Neaten

If the items that you no longer want are in relatively good condition, you could donate or sell them. If you have too many things that you're not going to use within the next couple of months, you can store your extras. Place donations in the box marked" Donations". Place the things you're going to sell in the box labeled "Sale". Place the things you're going to store in the box marked "Storage". Put the things you're going to get rid of in the trash bag, and put your recyclables in another bag.

Assign

Cluster the remaining items into equipment, or items that are used for a specific sport or recreational activity. So, you may end up with a pile of biking equipment, pool accessories, skating equipment, tennis equipment, etc.

Place

You can hang almost all of your equipment. You can install wall hooks or install pegboard to mount your items on. You can also place them on shelves or put them in cupboards. Remember, try to keep the floor clear. This is because a garage is for your car; so make sure you have space to park it.

Garden Accessories

Sort

The first thing you should do is fish out your garden accessories and place them in a central location. Go through it, and put all the things that you no longer want or need into a single pile.

You will then be left with two piles: one that has the things that you want, and the other will consist of things you don't want.

Neaten

If the items that you no longer want are in relatively good condition, you could donate or sell them. If you have too many things that you're not going to use within the next couple of months, you can store your extras. Place donations in the box marked "Donations". Place the things you're going to sell in the box labeled "Sale". Place the things you're going to store in the box marked "Storage". Put the things you're going to get rid of in the trash bag, and put your recyclables in another bag.

Assign

Divide the remaining things into like items. If you have a bunch of gardening tools, group those together, then gather all of your hoses and nozzles together. Continue to group all of your other garden items together until they are all in their respective piles.

Place

You now need to find homes for all these wonderful things that you've collected. You may need to invest in a hose organizer, storage containers, or bins. You can also install cupboards and shelves to house these items.

Tip

You can paint the walls as a way of brightening up the space.

SNAP the Boxes

Now, it's time to SNAP the bags and boxes.

Sort

Put all the packed bags together, and put all the packed boxes together.

Neaten

Put all the Storage boxes together, all the Donation boxes together, and all the Sale boxes together. Now, group all the trash bags together, and do the same with recyclables.

Assign and Place

Put all the trash bags in the garbage can, and the recyclables in the recycle bin.

Place the Sale boxes in the garage, or designate an area that is out of the way. Make sure that you can easily access them when you're ready to have your sale.

You can load the Donation boxes in your car, so you can drive them to the thrift store. If you've rented a storage unit, you can place the Storage boxes in the car and drive them to the storage unit, as well. If you plan on storing them at home, make sure they are out of the way and neatly stacked.

Reward

You may want to take some time out to enjoy your sports equipment; now that you can find it. So, if you play tennis, take an hour out of your schedule to visit the court. After all, you're entitled to treat yourself for this selfless act of kindness that you've done for your car!

Scent

You can place some potpourri in small bags or containers in the garage. That way, the garage will always smell great!

Maintenance

Clean out your garage every season, and get rid of anything that is broken or not being used.

Online Resource

Visit www.organizetosell.com for helpful tips and advice. You can also sign up for giveaways and contests too. This site was built with you in mind, so feel free to email your questions.

Joy Rich, LL.B.

Box List

Room Name:

Box #	Description of Contents

Box List

Room Name:

Box #	Description of Contents

Joy Rich, LL.B.

Notes:

Notes:

Kitchen: Before Picture

Kitchen: After Picture

Chapter 3
Kitchen

Kitchens sell houses. So, you need to make sure your kitchen is in tip-top condition when you put it on the market. But have no fear, by following the SNAP guidelines, you can tackle any mess. You need to sort, neaten, assign, and place all the items in your kitchen. It sounds easy, doesn't it? Just follow these instructions, and before you know it, your kitchen will be spotless.

SNAP the Kitchen

Before you start, take a picture of the room. The before picture will allow you to see what you don't want the room to look like again. There's a blank page at the beginning of the chapter for before and after pictures. Before you begin organizing the kitchen, make sure you have everything you need. Here's a check list of everything you'll need:

1. A marker
2. A pen
3. Packaging tape
4. Scissors
5. A box for Donations
6. A box for Sale items
7. A box for Storage items
8. A garbage bag
9. A bag for recyclables

10. This book
11. Extra boxes and bags

Once a box is full, you should:

1. Tape it closed.
2. Assign it a number.
3. Write the room's name on it (for example: kitchen).
4. Write a short description of its contents on it (for example: dishes).
5. Fill out the Box List at the end of each chapter when you've completed the room. This will allow you to keep track of all your boxes in one place. As well, because the list is in the book, you won't misplace it!

At the end of each chapter, there is a "Notes" section. You can use this for any notes you may need to make while packing, or for things you will need to do while unpacking. Make sure to take an after picture, and place it at the beginning of the chapter below the before picture. The after picture will set a standard for you to maintain.

Countertops

I suggest that you start with your countertop. This will allow you to utilize the clear counter space to better organize the rest of the kitchen.

Sort

Put all the dirty dishes, pans, utensils, glasses, cups, and anything else that needs to be washed, in the sink. Throw out anything that may be rotting, empty, or inedible. Gather all the kitchen towels, aprons, and oven mitts into a pile.

Neaten

Throw all of the kitchen towels, oven mitts, and aprons into the washing machine; these are in dire need of cleaning. Wash all the dirty dishes and anything else that you can get your hands on. Wipe down the countertop with soap and water, and then dry it.

Assign

Wipe the dishes and categorize them. Place all the like items into stacks or groups. You should end up with a stack of plates, bowls, saucers, pots, and groups of spoons, knives, forks, glasses, and cups, etc.

Place

You may need to leave these items on the counter for the time being, until you organize your cupboards. After your cupboards have been organized, remember less is more. Keep your counter tops as naked as possible. Try to keep the things you have on them down to a minimum.

Tip

Try to avoid buying things that you keep on the counter, such as knife sets, utensil holders, spoon sets, etc.

Cupboards
Dishes
Sort

Take all the dishes out of your cupboards. You can categorize them into piles of dishes that you use, and dishes that you don't use.

Neaten

If the items that you no longer want are in relatively good condition, you can donate or sell them. If you have too many things that you're not going to use within the next couple of months, you can store your extras. Place donations in the box marked "Donations". Place the things you're going to sell in the box labeled "Sale". Place the things you're going to store in the box marked "Storage". Put the things you're going to get rid of in the trash bag, and put your recyclables in another bag.

Assign

Place all the like items into similar piles. You will then end up with stacks of dishes, bowls, saucers, and groups of glasses and cups.

Place

You should group your plates, glasses, and cups that you use on a daily basis together, and have them in a convenient location so they can be easy to reach. This will make it rather effortless to put away after they have been washed. As well, you should keep your fine dining plates in another location. Since you don't use them regularly, they don't have to be easily accessible. So, you can use the shelves that are higher up in the cupboards; or in other words, the ones that no one can reach.

Pots, Pans and Storage Containers
Sort

Locate all of your pots, pans, and storage containers, and put them in a central location. Separate them into two groups. One group will consist of pots and pans that you want to keep, because they are still in good condition and you want to continue using them. The storage containers that will go in this pile all still have their matching lids and have no holes in them, nor have they been melted because of overheating. The other pile will have the pots, pans, and storage containers that you no longer want.

Neaten

If the items that you no longer want are in relatively good condition, you could donate or sell them. If you have too many things that you're not going to use within the next couple of months, you can store your extras. Place donations in the box marked "Donations". Place the things you're going to sell in the box labeled "Sale". Place the things you're going to store in the box marked "Storage". Put the things you're going to get rid of in the trash bag, and put your recyclables in another bag.

Assign

The items that remain need to be put into like groups. Therefore, you will end up with groups of frying pans, sauce pans, stock pots, etc., along with their matching lids. Your storage containers should be stacked into similar types along with their matching lids.

Place

Your pots and pans should be kept away from your Tupperware. You need to categorize them and stack them in a convenient way. For example, if you use your frying pan and sauce pan often, keep those together in the front of the cupboard. If you use your slow cooker once a month, then you can put that in the back. As well, if you use small storage containers often, then place those in the front of the cupboard, and the bigger ones can go towards the back of the cupboard.

Spices, Canned items, and Other Food Items
Sort

Pull all of your food items out of the cupboards, and place them on your counter top. Take a quick glance at all the items. Pull out all the open stale bags of chips or other snacks that have been opened for a while, and throw them out. Comb through the vitamins and painkillers, and check their expiration date. If they are past due, discard them. Take a look at the canned food, and pull anything that you will not use and put them in a pile. You may have canned soups, canned vegetables, and some other things that you may have bought and have never used, and may never use.

Neaten

The items that you will not be using can be donated to your local **FOOD BANK**. This will definitely warm someone's soul. So, place them in your donation box.

Assign

The remaining items you can section into piles of like items. For example, you may end up with groups of canned soups, spices, canned vegetables, snacks, vitamins, etc.

Place

Make things easy to reach by placing the things that you use the most in the front of the cupboards. Use separate cupboards for spices, canned goods, staples, snacks, vitamins, etc. This will enable you to find things easily and quickly based on what category it falls under.

Kitchen Drawers
Utensils and Gadgets
Sort

Pull all the utensils and gadgets out of their hiding places, and put them on your countertop. Put all the utensils into two piles. The first pile will consist of things you want and use. The second pile will contain the things that are bent or broken. Do the same with your gadgets, and add a third category that consists of things that you no longer want.

Neaten

If the items that you no longer want are in relatively good condition, you can donate or sell them. If you have too many things that you're not going to use within the next couple of months, you can store your extras. Place donations in the box marked "Donations". Place the things you're going to sell in the box labeled "Sale". Place the things you're going to store in the box marked "Storage". Put the things you're going to get rid of in the trash bag, and put your recyclables in another bag.

Assign

The remaining items can be divided into different groups of like items. For example, you will end up with groups of forks, knives, spoons, cooking spoons, serving spoons, spatulas, can openers, etc.

Place

Keep your everyday utensils separate from the utensils that you cook with. You should put them in two separate drawers. Place your kitchen gadgets, such as your can openers, wine openers, pizza cutter, etc., in a separate drawer as well.

Placemats, Coasters, and Kitchen Towels
Sort

Gather all of your placemats, coasters, and kitchen towels together. Place all the items into two piles. The first will consist of things that you use and things that you want. The second will contain the items that you no longer want, and things that are tattered, torn, or have holes in them.

Neaten

If the items that you no longer want are in relatively good condition, you can donate or sell them. If you have too many things that you're not going to use within the next couple of months, you can store your extras. Place donations in the box marked "Donations". Place the things you're going to sell in the box labeled "Sale". Place the things you're going to store in the box marked "Storage". Put the things you're going to get rid of in the trash bag, and put your recyclables in another bag.

Assign

The remaining items can be divided into sections of like items. So, you will end up with groups of coasters, placemats, and kitchen towels.

Place

The best location for your coasters and placemats are in a drawer. This will enable them to be handy, but not in the way. You need to utilize another drawer for the towels, because they deserve a place in the kitchen.

Appliances
Sort

Seek out all the appliances that you have hidden in your kitchen. Divide them into appliances that you use, appliances that you don't want, and appliances that are broken.

Neaten

If the items that you no longer want are in relatively good condition, you can donate or sell them. If you have too many things that you're not going to use within the next couple of months, you can store your extras. Place donations in the box marked "Donations". Place the things you're going to sell in the box labeled "Sale". Place the things you're going to store in the box marked "Storage". Put the things you're going to get rid of in the trash bag, and put your recyclables in another bag.

Assign

Separate the remaining items into groups of like items, such as coffee makers, toasters, blenders, food processors, etc.

Place

Keep the amount of appliances that you have on the counter to a minimum. This will eliminate the appearance of clutter. That would mean that you will have to segregate a cupboard for storing your precious food processors, blenders, toasters, etc.

Freezer

Sort

Start with your freezer. Take everything out, and sort everything into two piles: items that have not been freezer burned, and items that are freezer burned. Remember the garbage can is your friend, so go ahead and use it! Throw the freezer burned items away.

Neaten

You need to sort the remaining items into things that you will use and things that you will not use. Chances are, if they have been there for a long time, you will not use them. Throw away the things you will not use.

Assign

Divide the remaining items into like groups. For example: frozen fruits, frozen vegetables, frozen chicken, etc.

Place

You can categorize the items in the freezer according to the type of meat, fish, or entree it is. You can place all the chicken and other white meats on one shelf, red meats on another shelf, and all your frozen entrees on a separate shelf. If you have a single compartment freezer, follow the same guidelines and group the items together. You can buy small plastic bins to store the different items in. For example, you can have a bin that contains all of your frozen fruits.

Fridge

Sort

Start by emptying out all the contents of your fridge. Throw away rotting fruits and vegetables, as well as any bread or cheese that have grown mold on them. Remember, when in doubt, throw it out!

Neaten

Go through everything that has an expiration date on it, and if it's past due, then throw it out. If you have any food storage containers in the fridge, you should open them up and throw out their contents. As for take-out containers, you should completely discard it; container and all. Once everything is out of the fridge, you need to wipe it down with soap and water, and then dry it.

Assign

The remaining items need to be categorized into like items, such as beverages, fruits, vegetables, leftovers, etc.

Place

Designate the shelves in the fridge for a specific group of items. For instance, use the top shelf for breads and eggs, the middle shelf for leftovers, the third shelf for dairy products, and the shelves on the door for sauces, etc.

SNAP the Boxes

Now, it's time to SNAP the bags and boxes.

Sort

Put all the packed bags together, and put all the packed boxes together.

Neaten

Put all the Storage boxes together, all the Donation boxes together, and all the Sale boxes together. Now, group all the trash bags together and all the bags with recyclables together.

Assign and Place

You can put all the trash bags in the garbage can and the recyclables in the recycle bin.

Place the Sale boxes in the garage, or designate an area that is out of the way. Make sure that you can easily access them when you're ready to have your sale. You can load the Donation boxes in your car, so you can drive them to the thrift store. If you've rented a storage unit, you can place the Storage boxes in the car and drive them to the storage unit, as well. If you plan on storing them at home, make sure they are out of the way and neatly stacked.

Tip

Magnetic pad

Place a magnetic pad on the fridge, so that you will be able to write down all the things that you run out of or need. Then, when you go the grocery store, you will know exactly what to buy.

Reward

Now that you have done the impossible and organized your kitchen, it's time to eat some cake!

Scent

You should put a box of baking soda in the fridge to absorb the odors.

Maintenance

Go through the fridge every month. Make sure that you throw out old and expired food. Go through kitchen cupboards once a month, and check expiration dates on your items and discard accordingly. You can also throw out stale snacks that have been sitting there for a while.

Online Resource

Visit www.organizetosell.com for helpful tips and advice. You can also sign up for giveaways and contests too. This site was built with you in mind, so feel free to email your questions.

Box List

Room Name:

Box #	Description of Contents

Box List

Room Name:

Box #	Description of Contents

Joy Rich, LL.B.

Notes:

Notes:

Joy Rich, LL.B.

Living Room: Before Picture

Living Room: After Picture

Chapter 4
Living Room

The living room is usually one of the first rooms a potential buyer sees, so it needs to look appealing and inviting. Using the sorting, neatening, assigning, and placing (SNAP) method, you can straighten this room up quickly.

SNAP the Living Room

Before you start, take a picture of the room. The before picture will allow you to see what you don't want the room to look like again. There's a blank page at the beginning of the chapter for before and after pictures. Before you begin organizing the living room, make sure you have everything you need. Here's a check list of everything you'll need:

1. A marker
2. A pen
3. Packaging tape
4. Scissors
5. A box for Donations
6. A box for Sale items
7. A box for Storage items
8. A garbage bag
9. A bag for recyclables
10. This book
11. Extra boxes and bags

Once a box is full, you should:

1. Tape it closed.
2. Assign it a number.
3. Write the room's name on it (for example: kitchen).
4. Write a short description of its contents on it (for example: dishes).
5. Fill out the Box List at the end of each chapter when you've completed the room. This will allow you to keep track of all your boxes in one place. As well, because the list is in the book, you won't misplace it!

At the end of each chapter, there is a "Notes" section. You can use this for any notes you may need to make while packing, or for things you will need to do while unpacking. Make sure to take an after picture, and place it at the beginning of the chapter below the before picture. The after picture will set a standard for you to maintain.

Clothes, Blankets, and Cushions
Sort
One of the first items that need to be dealt with are the clothes. Collect all of them and place them in a central location. Get all the blankets and cushions, as well.

Neaten
Throw all the clothes and blankets into the washing machine.

Assign
Find an appropriate sofa for the small cushions. There should be enough cushions to add a splash of color to the sofa, and there should also be enough space for people to sit as well. Don't overcrowd the sofa.

Place
The blankets need to be placed in a strategic location, so they are easily accessible, as well as easy to put away. You can match the blanket to the

cushions, or the cushions to the blanket. You can spread a blanket along the top of the sofa, or simply throw it on the arm of the sofa.

Plates, Cups, Chips, Cookies, Popcorn, and Sodas
Sort
Gather all the plates, glasses, cups, spoons, and anything else that is food related, into a pile. Then, collect all of the snacks and drinks into another group.

Neaten
Take the plates, cups, and other utensils into the kitchen and wash them. The snacks and drinks can be thrown out.

Assign and Place
These things belong in the kitchen, and should be kept there. (See the section on Kitchens).

Magazines, Newspapers, and Books
Sort
Gather all of the magazines, newspapers, and books into a central location. You may need to put them into two piles: one consisting of the things that you want, and the other pile will have the things that you don't want.

Neaten
If the items that you no longer want are in relatively good condition, you could donate or sell them. If you have too many things that you're not going to use within the next couple of months, you can store your extras. Place donations in the box marked "Donations". Place the things you're going to sell in the box labeled "Sale". Place the things you're going to store in the box marked "Storage". Put the things you're going to get rid of in the trash bag, and put your recyclables in another bag.

Assign

The remaining items that you want to keep, you can divide up into like piles. You will end up with a pile of books and a group of magazines.

Place

Finding a home for these items is vital. You may want to invest in a magazine rack to house them in. You may even want to purchase a bookshelf, depending on how many books you want to keep in the living room. You may want to place a few on the coffee or side table to act as a conversation piece, or for guests to browse through.

Games, Remotes, CDs, and DVDs
Sort

Round up all of your games (electronic or board), remotes, CDs, and DVDs. You can then pull out the damaged or broken ones and discard them.

Neaten

If the items that you no longer want are in relatively good condition, you can donate or sell them. If you have too many things that you're not going to use within the next couple of months, you can store your extras. Place donations in the box marked "Donations". Place the things you're going to sell in the box labeled "Sale". Place the things you're going to store in the box marked "Storage". Put the things you're going to get rid of in the trash bag, and put your recyclables in another bag.

Assign

Categorize these items into like piles. You will wind up with piles of board games, electronic games, remotes, CDs, and DVDs.

Place

You may need to invest in some storage containers for these items if you don't have enough space. You may need a DVD and CD holder. If you want, you can also install shelves to house these items. Your games may need to be stored in your media center. If you don't have one, you may need to purchase a chest, or of even a book shelf of some sort, to house them in. If you have a lot of remotes, you may want to purchase a remote box to keep all of them in. You can even put them in a small basket. That way, you will always be able to find them when you need them.

SNAP the Boxes

Now, it's time to SNAP the bags and boxes.

Sort

Put all the packed bags together, and put all the packed boxes together.

Neaten

Put all the Storage boxes together, all the Donation boxes together, and all the Sale boxes together. Now, group all the trash bags together, and all the bags with recyclables together.

Assign and Place

You can put all the trash bags in the garbage can and the recyclables in the recycle bin.

Place the Sale boxes in the garage, or designate an area that is out of the way. Make sure that you can easily access them when you're ready to have your sale.

You can load the Donation boxes in your car so you can drive them to the thrift store. If you've rented a storage unit, you can place the Storage boxes in the car, and drive them to the storage unit, as well. If you plan on storing them at home, make sure they are out of the way and neatly stacked.

Reward

Treat yourself to a movie now that you have tackled this room. You can either rent one, or go to the theatre.

Scent

Febreze air freshener is a great product to have on hand for this room. It can be used on upholstered furniture; so it'll keep your sofas smelling great! Keep it on hand and use it frequently.

Maintenance

Make sure that you spot check your living room once a week to keep it looking and smelling great.

Online Resource

Visit www.organizetosell.com for helpful tips and advice. You can also sign up for giveaways and contests too. This site was built with you in mind, so feel free to email your questions.

Box List

Room Name:

Box #	Description of Contents

Joy Rich, LL.B.

Notes:

Notes:

Dining Room: Before Picture

Dining Room: After Picture

Chapter 5
Dining Room

Dining rooms often become a problem area, because they are rarely used. This, as a result, makes it an easy target for clutter, because you may feel that you're putting things out of the way; but you're not. Buyers want to envision themselves having dinner parties and entertaining in this space. So, it's imperative that this space looks inviting. This can be accomplished in just four easy steps: sort, neaten, assign and place.

SNAP the Dining Room

Before you start, take a picture of the room. The before picture will allow you to see what you don't want the room to look like again. There's a blank page at the beginning of the chapter for before and after pictures. Before you begin organizing the dining room, make sure you have everything you need. Here's a check list of everything you'll need:

1. A marker
2. A pen
3. Packaging tape
4. Scissors
5. A box for Donations
6. A box for Sale items
7. A box for Storage items
8. A garbage bag
9. A bag for recyclables

10. This book
11. Extra boxes and bags

Once a box is full, you should:
1. Tape it closed.
2. Assign it a number.
3. Write the room's name on it (for example: kitchen).
4. Write a short description of its contents on it (for example: dishes).
5. Fill out the Box List at the end of each chapter when you've completed the room. This will allow you to keep track of all your boxes in one place. As well, because the list is in the book, you won't misplace it!

At the end of each chapter, there is a "Notes" section. You can use this for any notes you may need to make while packing, or for things you will need to do while unpacking. Make sure to take an after picture, and place it at the beginning of the chapter below the before picture. The after picture will set a standard for you to maintain.

Flat Wear, Utensils, and Serving Wear
Sort
Remove everything, but the dishes, utensils, and serving trays, off the table. Then take all of the dishes, cups, and glasses out of the display case. You should empty the display cabinet, because there may be things in there that you can store somewhere else. You should then go through all the items, and pull things out that are chipped or items that you no longer want. Place these in one pile.

Neaten
If the items that you no longer want are in relatively good condition, you can donate or sell them. If you have too many things that you're not going to use within the next couple of months, you can store your extras. Place donations in the box marked "Donations". Place the things you're going to sell in the

box labeled "Sale". Place the things you're going to store in the box marked "Storage". Put the things you're going to get rid of in the trash bag, and put your recyclables in another bag.

Assign

You can then start to group the items that you want to keep into two piles. The first group will consist of the items that you want to have in your display cabinet. The second group will consist of everything else.

Place

The items that you have chosen to display in your cabinet should be placed there. You can display them in a manner which reflects your personality! You may have to invest in some plate stands, if you don't have them already. If you have extra storage capacity in the bottom of your display cabinet, you can place the remaining items there in their respective groups. If you have more than one pattern of plates, then keep them separate, but leave them in the pile of plates.

If you don't have enough storage for your items in the display cabinet, then you may have to add them to your kitchen cabinet collection. You can place them on the higher shelves, because they are not for everyday dining. If you have no more storage, then you may want to think about adding some more items to your flat ware sale.

Place mats, Coasters, and Table Clothes
Sort

Go through the room, pull these items out of there hiding places, and put them on the table.

Neaten

Put them into two piles. One pile will consist of things that you don't want any more, or are tattered and old. The items that are in relatively good condition, you can donate or sell. Place donations in the box marked "Donations". Place the things you're going to sell in the box labeled "Sale". Put the things you're going to get rid of in the trash bag, and put your recyclables in another bag.

The other pile will consist of things that you want to keep. If you have too many things that you're not going to use within the next couple of months, you can store your extras. Place the things you're going to store in the box marked "Storage".

Assign

Place the items you're keeping into piles of similar items. You will, therefore, end up with groups of place mats, coasters, and table clothes.

Place

Find a place for these items. You may have space for them in your cabinet, if it has drawers. If not, then you may place them in your kitchen with the other place mats and coasters.

Miscellaneous Items

Sort

Go through all the items and pull out the things that you no longer want. If these items are not worth keeping, or are broken, then you should throw them out.

Neaten

If the items that you no longer want are in relatively good condition, you can donate or sell them. If you have too many things that you're not going to use within the next couple of months, you can store your extras. Place donations in the box marked "Donations". Place the things you're going to sell in the box labeled "Sale". Place the things you're going to store in the box marked "Storage". Put the things you're going to get rid of in the trash bag, and put your recyclables in another bag.

Assign

Categorize these items into piles of like items.

Place

The remaining items that you are left with need homes. If you have gift paper, then you will need to place them in a container with the bows and boxes, and maybe store them in a closet or the basement. You may need to label the container, if it is not transparent. As for the books, you can place them on a bookshelf and put them in your study, or even in your living room. Do the same with the remaining items; group them, find an appropriate container, and then put them away.

Tips

Make sure that your storage goes with your décor. For example, if you add a bookshelf to a room, you can paint it to match the surroundings. Remember, less is more! You should keep the items on the table to a minimum. You can have a few candle sticks and a bowl on the table, or a nice arrangement of flowers. You can also have a runner going down the center of the table for a touch of elegance. If you don't want your dining room to look bare, then you should hang some art work on the walls for an instant make-over.

SNAP the Boxes

Now, it's time to SNAP the bags and boxes.

Sort

Put all the packed bags together, and put all the packed boxes together.

Neaten

Put all the Storage boxes together, all the Donation boxes together, and all the Sale boxes together. Now, group all the trash bags together, and all the bags with recyclables together.

Assign and Place

You can put all the trash bags in the garbage can and the recyclables in the recycle bin.

Place the Sale boxes in the garage, or designate an area that is out of the way. Make sure that you can easily access them when you're ready to have your sale.

You can load the Donation boxes in your car, so you can drive them to the thrift store. If you've rented a storage unit, you can place the Storage boxes in the car, and drive them to the storage unit, as well. If you plan on storing them at home, make sure they are out of the way and neatly stacked.

Reward

Organizing this room is a huge accomplishment! Make sure you celebrate with a nice meal. You can cook it yourself, or go out to a restaurant.

Scent

You should add a plug-in air freshener to this space to keep it smelling great at all times. Choose something fruity to keep with the theme of eating. After all, that is what this room was meant for.

Maintenance

Make sure that you keep things in their designated places. When you use something, return it to its home. Spot check your dining room every couple of weeks to make sure that your table and floor are clear.

Online Resource

Visit www.organizetosell.com for helpful tips and advice. You can also sign up for giveaways and contests too. This site was built with you in mind, so feel free to email your questions.

Box List

Room Name:

Box #	Description of Contents

Joy Rich, LL.B.

Notes:

Notes:

Bathroom: Before Picture

Bathroom: After Picture

Chapter 6
Bathroom

The bathroom is a high traffic area, which as a result, can easily become chaotic. Buyers want clean bathrooms that look and smell good. Luckily for you, this can be done easily in just four steps by using the SNAP method.

SNAP the Bathroom

Before you start, take a picture of the room. The before picture will allow you to see what you don't want the room to look like again. There's a blank page at the beginning of the chapter for before and after pictures. Before you begin organizing a room, make sure you have everything you need. Here's a check list of everything you'll need:

1. A marker
2. A pen
3. Packaging tape
4. Scissors
5. A box for Donations
6. A box for Sale items
7. A box for Storage items
8. A garbage bag
9. A bag for recyclables
10. This book
11. Extra boxes and bags

Once a box is f, you should:

1. Tape it closed.
2. Assign it a number.
3. Write the room's name on it (for example: kitchen).
4. Write a short description of its contents on it (for example: dishes).
5. Fill out the Box List at the end of each chapter when you've completed the room. This will allow you to keep track of all your boxes in one place. As well, because the list is in the book, you won't misplace it!

At the end of each chapter, there is a "Notes" section. You can use this for any notes you may need to make while packing, or for things you will need to do while unpacking. Make sure to take an after picture, and place it at the beginning of the chapter below the before picture. The after picture will set a standard for you to maintain.

Bathroom Cupboards
Sort
Pull all of the items out of your cupboards and put them in two piles. The first pile will have the things that are still usable. The second pile will have things that are expired, or things that you no longer want or need.

Neaten
If you haven't used something for three months, throw it out. Check expiration dates on products. If it's past the due date, throw it out! If you have too many things that you're not going to use within the next couple of months, you can store your extras, so put them in the "Storage" box. Put the things you're going to get rid of in the trash bag, and your recyclables in another bag.

Assign
Put the items in the cupboards in groups. For example, group hair products together, feminine items together, medications together, eye care products together, etc.

Place

You may need to buy storage bins to store these items in. For example, your eye care products can go in one container, your feminine products can go in another, and your medications can go in one. You can use stackable containers with drawers that pull out, as well as baskets. The choice is yours.

Bathroom Counter

Sort

If you have too many things on the counter, it looks cluttered. Pick through it and throw out anything that is empty or expired.

Neaten

Eliminate as much as possible off the countertop. You should sort your items by gathering everything on your counter to a central location. Put the items into two piles: one consisting of hand soap, hand cream, and air freshener; the other pile will consist of everything else. Put the things you're going to get rid of in the trash bag, or if you're going to recycle it, put it in the recyclable bag. If you have too many things that you're not going to use within the next couple of months, you can put them in storage, so place it in its respective box.

Assign

You should just have your bathroom staples on the counter. These are items such as hand soap, cream, and an air freshener. This will take care of one pile. Make sure that you don't have too many different kinds of hand soaps, creams, and air fresheners. One is enough to start off with. Place the rest in the remaining pile. Then, start categorizing the items from the pile that remains. You will end up with several groups of things: such as toothpaste, razors, deodorants, etc.

Place

You can then place the items in the cupboards in their designated area (if you have already arranged your cupboards. If you have not, then you need to).

Remember, you may need to invest in bins, baskets, or stackable containers to keep your things in order.

Towels, Clothes, and Mats

Sort

Gather all of these items on the floor.

Neaten

Most likely, if they are on your bathroom floor, they need to be washed. So, put them all in your hamper. Make sure that your bathroom mats can be easily washed. These need to visit the washing machine often.

Tip

I love tub mats, because you can throw them in the machine when you wash your towels.

Assign

The first thing that you're going to have to do is find an appropriate place for your towels and clothing, such as robes.

Place

Make sure that there are sufficient towel bars, or hooks, in the bathroom for your bath towels, hand towels, and robes. You don't want to have your towels being thrown over the shower curtain bar, or hanging on the door handle. That's definitely a big NO-NO! You can place hooks behind your bathroom door for extra storage, as well as install additional towel bars to do the job. You should place at least one mat in the bathroom near to the tub to step on when coming out of the shower. This is to ensure that you don't slip on the floor when stepping out of the tub.

Hampers

Sort

If you send your clothes to the dry cleaners, make sure that you have two different hampers. Designate one for machine washables, and one for the dry cleaners.

Neaten

Having a hamper isn't enough to keep your clothes off the ground; you actually have to use it. Make sure that you place your dirty clothes in the hampers. If you want to keep the place neat and clean, then you also have to do laundry on a regular basis. So, wash the clothes in the hamper.

Assign

If one hamper is for your dry cleaning, and one is for your machine washables, then place the appropriate item in the appropriate hamper.

Place

Placing a hamper in a strategic location is vital to its usage. If your guests have access to your bathroom, then you may need to keep your hampers in the bedroom.

Tub and Shower Area

Sort

Like most people's homes, the tub area is overflowing with soaps, shampoos, scrubs, etc. Gather all of these things into a central location. Place them into two piles. The first will consist of things that you don't want, and things that you have finished. The second pile will contain things that you want and use.

Neaten

Throw out or recycle the items that are empty, or that you no longer want. If you have too many things that you're not going to use within the next couple of months, you should store them. Place them in the storage box.

Assign

Assign the remaining piles into like items. You will end up with a pile of soap, shampoos, bubble baths, etc. Keep the number of soaps, shampoos, and bubble baths to a limit.

Place

You may have to invest in an organizer that you can hang over the shower. If the remaining items are too plentiful to fit in the organizer, you may have to further eliminate items. Keep the shampoos and soaps to a minimum. If there are any excess items, put them away. You can use them when the products that you are currently using run out.

Tip

It's often tempting to put a gift set that someone gave you in your bathroom. However, if your bathroom is already stocked, put the gift set up, and use it when your current supplies are finished.

SNAP the Boxes

Now, it's time to SNAP the bags and boxes.

Sort

Put all the packed bags together, and put all the packed boxes together.

Neaten

Put all the Storage boxes together, all the Donation boxes together, and all the Sale boxes together. Now, group all the trash bags together, and all the bags with recyclables together.

Assign and Place

You can put all the trash bags in the garbage can, and the recyclables in the recycle bin.

Place the Sale boxes in the garage, or designate an area that is out of the way. Make sure that you can easily access them when you're ready to have your sale.

You can load the Donation boxes in your car, so you can drive them to the thrift store. If you've rented a storage unit, you can place the Storage boxes in the car, so you can drive them to the storage unit, as well. If you plan on storing them at home, make sure they are out of the way and neatly stacked.

Reward
Now that you have finally tidied up this room, treat yourself to a nice bubble bath!

Scent
It is a good idea to keep a can of disinfectant spray in the bathroom. These come in various scents, so they can double as an air freshener.

Maintenance
Clean your bathroom cupboards out every three months. Make it a point to get rid of anything that you are not using, or anything that has expired.

Online Resource
Visit www.organizetosell.com for helpful tips and advice. You can also sign up for giveaways and contests too. This site was built with you in mind, so feel free to email your questions.

Box List

Room Name:

Box #	Description of Contents

Box List

Room Name:

Box #	Description of Contents

Joy Rich, LL.B.

Notes:

Notes:

Bedroom: Before Picture

Bedroom: After Picture

Chapter 7
Bedrooms

Buyers want big, spacious bedrooms. However, bedrooms often become havens for everything that one owns. So, you need to make the room appear spacious and appealing. You can do this in a SNAP.

SNAP the Bedrooms

Before you start, take a picture of the room. The before picture will allow you to see what you don't want the room to look like again. There's a blank page at the beginning of the chapter for before and after pictures. Before you begin organizing a room, make sure you have everything you need. Here's a check list of everything you'll need:

1. A marker
2. A pen
3. Packaging tape
4. Scissors
5. A box for Donations
6. A box for Sale items
7. A box for Storage items
8. A garbage bag
9. A bag for recyclables
10. This book
11. Extra boxes and bags

Once a box is full, you should:

1. Tape it closed.
2. Assign it a number.
3. Write the room's name on it (for example: kitchen).
4. Write a short description of its contents on it (for example: dishes).
5. Fill out the Box List at the end of each chapter when you've completed the room. This will allow you to keep track of all your boxes in one place. As well, because the list is in the book, you won't misplace it!

At the end of each chapter, there is a "Notes" section. You can use this for any notes you may need to make while packing, or for things you will need to do while unpacking. Make sure to take an after picture, and place it at the beginning of the chapter below the before picture. The after picture will set a standard for you to maintain.

Clothing
Sort
You can start digging yourself out by using the sorting method. This is where you put everything in a pile. You can pull them out of the drawers and off the hangers in order to do a thorough job. You then separate them into two piles: things you no longer want, and things that you want. Remember the rule of thumb: if it's old, tattered, or broken, it should be thrown out.

Tip
Keep the things that make you feel good. If something is too small or too big, eliminate it from your collection.

Neaten
Now, you will start to neaten up the pile by combing through the things you no longer want. The items that are in relatively good condition, you can donate or sell. If you have too many things that you're not going to use within the next couple of months, you can store your extras. Place donations in

the box marked "Donations". Place the things you're going to sell in the box labeled "Sale". Place the things you're going to store in the box marked "Storage". Put the things you're going to get rid of in the trash bag, and put your recyclables in another bag.

Assign

You should then assign the remaining clean clothes into two piles: clothes you wear outside the house, and clothes that you wear around the house (for example: pajamas). So, you will end up with a pile of:

T-shirts (subdivide into house clothes and outside wear)

Pajamas

Robes

Shirts (sub-divide into work, formal, and casual)

Pants (subdivide into dressy and casual)

Dresses (subdivide into formal and casual)

Skirts (sub-divide into dressy, casual, and work)

Jackets (subdivide these into dressy, suits jackets, sports jackets, and casual)

Sweaters (subdivide into dressy, casual and work)

Place

Now, you have to find a home for all of your clothes. You can start by figuring out what item you wear most often. If you wear pants and shirts most often, then these items should be put in a location that will enable you to have easy access to them. You may, therefore, want to place them in the front of your closet. If you hardly wear dresses, then they should go to the back of your closet. You will then need to figure out what you want to put in drawers, and what you want to hang in the closet. You can put items like clothes that you wear at home in drawers, and leave the closet available for things that you wear out. Make sure that you don't overcrowd your drawers or closet. You may need additional storage for your things, so you may consider getting another dresser or sweater chest. Remember, because of the large selection of storage items available to you in the stores, you can get something that blends in with your decor.

Socks and Underwear
Sort

You need to pull all of these items out of the drawers or off the floor, and closely examine them. Put them into two piles. The first pile will consist of things that you want. The second pile will contain the things that you no longer want. The things that you don't want, you can throw out.

Neaten

If the items that you no longer want are in relatively good condition, you can donate or sell them. If you have too many things that you're not going to use within the next couple of months, you can store your extras. Place donations in the box marked "Donations". Place the things you're going to sell in the box labeled "Sale". Place the things you're going to store in the box marked "Storage". Put the things you're going to get rid of in the trash bag, and put your recyclables in another bag.

Assign

The remaining items can then be categorized. Put them into piles of like items, such as:

Socks (subdivide into dressy and casual)

Pantyhose

Bras (subdivide into sporty and regular)

Underwear (subdivide into panties, briefs, etc.)

Undershirts (subdivide into t-shirt and armless).

Place

These items should all be given their own drawers. If you have big drawers and want to place a few of these items in the same drawer, you may need to buy containers that fit easily into the drawer to separate the items. For example, if you are going to place socks and pantyhose in one drawer, you may need to buy two bins that fit into the drawer: one for your panty hose, and one for your socks. If you have too many things that you're not going to use within the next couple of months, you can store your extras. Place the things you're going to store in the box marked "Storage". Put the things you're going to get rid of in the trash bag, and put your recyclables in another bag.

Coats and Outer Wear Accessories
Sort

Over time, one tends to accumulate a lot of clothes and accessories. Scarf sets seem to have increased in popularity over the past few years, and as a result, you may have ended up with quite a few of them. First of all, you need to take inventory of all of your coats and accessories. Put them in two piles. The first will contain the things that are old, ripped, outdated, or things that you no longer want. The second will consist of the things you want.

Neaten

Discard the things that are ripped or torn. If the items that you no longer want are in relatively good condition, you can donate or sell them. If you have too many things that you're not going to use within the next couple of months, you can store your extras. Place donations in the box marked "Donations". Place the things you're going to sell in the box labeled "Sale". Place the things you're going to store in the box marked "Storage". Put the things you're going to get rid of in the trash bag, and put your recyclables in another bag.

Assign

The items that you want will need to be categorized. Most people just push their coats into the closet and leave it at that. However, it's a lot more effective if you categorize them by season and usage. You can start by categorizing them into winter, fall, spring, and summer. Once you have them in these piles, you can then further subdivide them into dressy and casual. Remember to also catalog your outer wear accessories, like your hats, scarves, gloves, and umbrellas. Once you have these in different piles, you can put them with their corresponding coats. Therefore, you will have your winter accessories with your winter coats, your spring accessories, like umbrellas, with your spring coats, and so on.

Place

You can put your coats that are out of season in the back of your closet. The accessories that correspond with them can be placed on the shelf above them in the closet. You can buy a basket or container to place them in. If you buy stackable containers, you can label them. For example, winter accessories, spring accessories, etc.

Ties, Belts, Scarves, Hats, and Handkerchiefs
Sort

Everyone has a bunch of accessories, but sometimes we have too many. Oh well, we just have to find a way to accommodate them in our homes. So, gather them all together in a central location and then start sorting them into piles of like items. You will have mounds of belts, scarves, ties, hats, and handkerchiefs.

Neaten

You would then go through the piles one by one. If you have belts, ties, scarves, hats, and handkerchiefs that are torn, old, or tattered, then throw them out. If the items that you no longer want are in relatively good condition, you can donate or sell them. If you have too many things that you're not going to use within the next couple of months, you can store your extras. Place donations in the box marked "Donations". Place the things you're going to sell in the box labeled "Sale". Place the things you're going to store in the box marked "Storage". Put the things you're going to get rid of in the trash bag, and put your recyclables in another bag.

Place the remaining items in designated piles of:

Ties

Belts (subdivide into dressy and casual)

Hats (subdivide into dressy, casual, sporty, and fun)

Scarves

Handkerchiefs (subdivide into cotton and silk).

Place

You can buy a tie organizer for your ties. That way, you will be able to view them at a glance. You can then place the tie organizer in the closet near to your work shirts. Your scarves can get hung on an accessory hanger. You can have them near to your shirts and jackets. You can put your belts on an accessory hanger of some kind, as well. These can go in the closet near to your pants. Your dressy hats can be kept in the closet on the shelf in Hat boxes. Your sporty hats can be stacked on top of each other in a neat pile. Handkerchiefs can be placed in a drawer or in a box, and can be housed on the shelf above your jackets.

Shoes

Sort

Gather your shoes from every corner of the room. If you're a woman, you will most likely end up with a mountain of kicks.

Neaten

Go through the pile of shoes, and pull out all the shoes that are worn out and all the ones that you no longer want. If the items are in relatively good condition, you can donate or sell them. If you have too many things that you're not going to use within the next couple of months, you can store your extras. Place donations in the box marked "Donations". Place the things you're going to sell in the box labeled "Sale". Place the things you're going to store in the box marked "Storage". Put the things you're going to get rid of in the trash bag, and put your recyclables in another bag.

Assign

The shoes that you are left with will definitely need to be sub-divide into piles of dressy, casual, and fitness.

Place

You may need to invest in a shoe organizer of some sort. There are so many on the market now. You can buy shoe organizers that you hang behind the door, a shoe rack, or some other shoe holding device. Remember to keep your shoes in their designated categories.

Purses

Sort

Purses and bags are another weakness for many people. Find all the bags you have, and heap them together.

Neaten

Separate them into piles of bags that you want, and bags that you no longer want. If the bags that you no longer want are in relatively good condition, you can donate or sell them. If you have too many things that you're not going to use within the next couple of months, you can store your extras. Place donations in the box marked "Donations". Place the things you're going to sell in the box labeled "Sale". Place the things you're going to store in the box marked "Storage". Put the things you're going to get rid of in the trash bag, and put your recyclables in another bag.

Assign

You should separate your purses into piles of evening, work, and casual.

Place

You can put your purses on the shelf on top of your closet. However, depending on the number of purses you have, you may have to buy additional storage.

You can get hooks that you put behind your door, wall hooks, or you may want to invest in a book shelf that you can use to house your purse collection in.

Jewelry, Sunglasses, and Hair Accessories
Sort
Collect all your jewelry, sunglasses, and hair accessories together.

Neaten
Go through each pile, and pull out items that are broken or that you no longer want. Throw all the broken or damaged items out. If the items that you no longer want are in relatively good condition, you can donate or sell them. If you have too many things that you're not going to use within the next couple of months, you can store your extras. Place donations in the box marked "Donations". Place the things you're going to sell in the box labeled "Sale". Place the things you're going to store in the box marked "Storage". Put the things you're going to get rid of in the trash bag, and put your recyclables in another bag.

Assign
You will have to put the items that you're keeping into several small piles. So, you will have small piles of hair accessories (subdivide these into hair ties, hair pins and hair clips), jewelry (subdivide into costume jewelry and precious stones, gold, etc.), and sunglasses.

Place
Find an appropriate place for your hair accessories; you may have to invest in a storage bin of some sort. Your sunglasses will also need a home. You may need to install some shelves in your bedroom to accommodate your specs. Your jewelry commands a place of its own, so you will need to invest in jewelry boxes. You are going to need one for your precious stones, and one for your costume jewelry. You may need additional space for these treasure chests, so you can once again install some shelves for them.

Make-Up, Nail Files, Nail Polish, Perfumes, and Colognes
Sort

Some people have drawers filled with these small indulgences. Gather them in to a central location.

Neaten

Pick through them and put them, into two piles. The first pile will consist of all the empty bottles, used nail files, and old make-up. Throw these items out or recycle them. The second pile will then need to be neatened up.

Assign

Put all of your make-up into small piles of foundations, powders, eye shadows, eye liners, mascaras, blushes, lip liners, and lipsticks. Nail accessories are also plentiful, so put them into piles of nail files, nail clippers, manicure related items, and pedicure related items. Nail polishes can just be in a pile of their own. Nail polish remover and cotton balls should get their own piles. Perfumes and colognes deserve their own piles. Body sprays can be coupled with them, if you so desire. If you have too many things that you're not going to use within the next couple of months, you can store your extras. Place the things you're going to store in the box marked "Storage".

Place

You may need to place your make-up, nail polishes, nail files, nail polish remover, and cotton balls in a small baskets or container of some kind. These items can go on top of your vanity, or on your dresser. Your perfumes or colognes can also be placed on your vanity or dresser. However, if you do not have a lot of room, you may need to install some shelves for these items.

Hair Accessories
Sort

Collect all of your hair accessories, such as curling irons, blow dryers, steam curlers, flat irons, etc., and place them in a central location. Comb through them and create two piles: one with things that are broken or that you don't want any more, and the other consisting of items that you want to keep.

Neaten

If the items that you no longer want are in relatively good condition, you can donate or sell them. If you have too many things that you're not going to use within the next couple of months, you can store your extras. Place donations in the box marked "Donations". Place the things you're going to sell in the box labeled "Sale". Place the things you're going to store in the box marked "Storage". Put the things you're going to get rid of in the trash bag, and put your recyclables in another bag.

Assign

Hair accessories, such as curling irons, blow dryers, steam curlers, flat irons, etc., all need to be grouped together into their own piles. Over time, you may have collected more of these than you realize.

Place

You will definitely need a storage container for these valuables. You can store these on the shelf in your closet. If you run out of space at any time, you can invest in a book shelf or install some shelves for your accessories.

CDs, DVDs, Books, Magazines, Newspapers, Pens, and Remotes
Sort

These items should be gathered and placed in a pile.

Neaten

You should then separate them into two piles. One for broken CD's and DVD's, old pens, newspapers, and magazines, as well as things you no longer want. You should throw these items out or recycle them. If the items are in relatively good condition, you can donate or sell them. Place donations in the box marked "Donations". Place the things you're going to sell in the box labeled "Sale". Put the things you're going to get rid of in the trash bag, and put your recyclables in another bag. The second group will be made up of things that you want to hang on to. If you have too many things that you're not going to use within the next couple of months, you can store your extras. Place the things you're going to store in the box marked "Storage".

Assign

You should segregate the piles of items that you still want, into small piles of like items. You will end up with a pile of CD's, DVD's, magazines, newspapers, and pens.

Place

You may need to buy a CD and a DVD holder to keep your collection in. You could place your magazines on a magazine rack. If you have a bookshelf, then these items can all go on the bookshelf.

SNAP the Boxes

Now, it's time to SNAP the bags and boxes.

Sort

Put all the packed bags together, and put all the packed boxes together.

Neaten

Put all the Storage boxes together, all the Donation boxes together, and all the Sale boxes together. Now, group all the trash bags together, and all the bags with recyclables together.

Assign and Place

You can put all the trash bags in the garbage can and the recyclables in the recycle bin.

Place the Sale boxes in the garage, or designate an area that is out of the way. Make sure that you can easily access them when you're ready to have your sale.

You can load the Donation boxes in your car, so you can drive them to the thrift store. If you've rented a storage unit, you can place the Storage boxes in the car, and drive them to the storage unit, as well. If you plan on storing them at home, make sure they are out of the way and neatly stacked.

Reward

Now that you have finally slain this dragon, you can relax and take a nap!

Scent

Scented candles have become a necessity in almost every home. Make sure your bedroom has a few.

Maintenance

Checking the tops of your dresser drawers once a month will help you to keep the clutter down to a minimum. If there has been an accumulation of things, you can keep it under control. Put items in a designated place. Remember, surfaces should be as naked as possible, so only keep a few key items on the dresser.

Go through your drawers every three months, and throw away torn or tattered clothing. Keep the things that make you feel good. If something is too small or too big, eliminate it from your collection. If your socks or undergarments have countless holes in them, then it's time for them to go.

Online Resource

Visit www.organizetosell.com for helpful tips and advice. You can also sign up for giveaways and contests too. This site was built with you in mind, so feel free to email your questions.

Joy Rich, LL.B.

Box List

Room Name:

Box #	Description of Contents

Notes:

Kids Room: Before Picture

Kids Room: After Picture

Chapter 8
Kids Rooms

Kids' rooms are often messy, just because they're kids and are too busy playing to organize. Buyers want to see a spacious room that looks clean and smells clean. Using the SNAP method, you can attack any mess large or small. So, roll your sleeves up, and get ready to organize this space.

SNAP the Kids Room

Before you start, take a picture of the room. The before picture will allow you to see what you don't want the room to look like again. There's a blank page at the beginning of the chapter for before and after pictures. Before you begin organizing a room, make sure you have everything you need. Here's a check list of everything you'll need:

1. A marker
2. A pen
3. Packaging tape
4. Scissors
5. A box for Donations
6. A box for Sale items
7. A box for Storage items
8. A garbage bag
9. A bag for recyclables
10. This book
11. Extra boxes and bags

Once a box is full, you should:

1. Tape it closed.
2. Assign it a number.
3. Write the room's name on it (for example: kitchen).
4. Write a short description of its contents on it (for example: dishes).
5. Fill out the Box List at the end of each chapter when you've completed the room. This will allow you to keep track of all your boxes in one place. As well, because the list is in the book, you won't misplace it!

At the end of each chapter, there is a "Notes" section. You can use this for any notes you may need to make while packing, or for things you will need to do while unpacking. Make sure to take an after picture, and place it at the beginning of the chapter below the before picture. The after picture will set a standard for you to maintain.

Crayons, Markers, Paint, Bags, Paper, Notepads, Books, and Learning Materials
Sort

Go through everything and pull out all of the crayons, markers, paint, bags, paper, notepads, books, and learning materials. Then, sort them into two groups. The first group will consist of things that the kids don't use, and things that are old, broken, or no longer fit. The second group will consist of things that the kids currently use.

Neaten

If the items that you no longer want are in relatively good condition, you can donate or sell them. If they have too many things that they're not going to use within the next couple of months, you can store your extras. Place donations in the box marked "Donations". Place the things you're going to sell in the box labeled "Sale". Place the things you're going to store in the box marked "Storage". Put the things you're going to get rid of in the trash bag, and put your recyclables in another bag.

Assign

You will need to categorize the remaining items. Group them into like items, such as crayons, pens, pencils, paints, book, notebooks, bags, etc.

Place

You may need to invest in a desk and bookshelf, if you don't already have one for the room. You can then place the books and notebooks on the bookshelf. Try to assign separate shelves for separate items. For example, the leisure reading books can go on one shelf, and the school books can go on a separate shelf. The painting materials, as well, can get their own shelf. The writing tools can go in a drawer in the desk. Try to keep as much of the surface of the desk clear, because it will give them more space to work on. Try to find an appropriate place for back packs. You can install a hook on the wall for the bag to be hung on, or you can put it on the floor beside the desk. It is essential that your child's room have a bulletin board. This way, they can tack up all of their assignments, schedules, and anything else they want. This can go above the desk for easy access.

Tip

If you don't have enough floor space for a bookshelf, you can install a few shelves on the wall to house the books. You can even run a countertop along the wall that can act as a desk.

Toys
Sort

Gather all the toys into a central location. Put them into two piles. One pile will have the toys that are broken or are no longer being used. The other pile will have toys that are still being used.

Neaten

If the items that you no longer want are in relatively good condition, you can donate or sell them. If they have too many things that they're not going to use within the next couple of months, you can store your extras. Place donations in the box marked "Donations". Place the things you're going to sell in the box labeled "Sale". Place the things you're going to store in the box marked "Storage". Put the things you're going to get rid of in the trash bag, and put your recyclables in another bag.

Assign

The remaining items need to be categorized into different types of toys. You will have a group of stuffed toys, trucks, dolls, puzzles, board games, etc.

Place

You can buy stackable storage containers that pull out from the front, and put the toys in there. You can also look for storage bins that pull out to fit under the bed. That will enable the containers to be out of the way, but easily accessible.

Sports Equipment
Sort

Gather all the sporting equipment into a central location. Go through this pile, and pull out the items that are no longer being used or have been outgrown. The items that are old and tattered can be thrown out. The items that are currently being used, and are in good condition, can go into a separate group.

Neaten

If the items that you no longer want are in relatively good condition, you can donate or sell them. If they have too many things that they're not going to use within the next couple of months, you can store your extras. Place donations in the box marked "Donations". Place the things you're going to sell in the box labeled "Sale". Place the things you're going to store in the box marked "Storage". Put the things you're going to get rid of in the trash bag, and put your recyclables in another bag.

Assign

The sporting gear needs to be divided into groups of items that are used for a particular activity. You will end up with a group of hockey gear, tennis gear, baseball gear, etc.

Place

These things definitely need a home. You can designate a particular area in the room for them. You may want to install some shelves that you can place items, such as gloves and helmets, on. You can also have hooks put on the wall to secure rackets or skates. You can also buy a tall bin to store hockey sticks or baseball bats in. That will ensure that they remain in their home and don't fall on the floor. You can display their awards and trophies on the same wall with a few additional shelves.

Music Equipment

Sort

Go through everything in the room, and bring all of the music related items together. That includes head phones, CDs, sheet music, and instruments.

Neaten

If the items that you no longer want are in relatively good condition, you can donate or sell them. If you have too many things that you're not going to use within the next couple of months, you can store your extras. Place donations in the box marked "Donations". Place the things you're going to sell in the box labeled "Sale". Place the things you're going to store in the box marked "Storage". Put the things you're going to get rid of in the trash bag, and put your recyclables in another bag.

Assign

Place similar items into piles of their own. You will end up with groups of CDs, sheet music, music stands, instruments, books, etc.

Place

You will need to designate an area in the room as an area for your child to play their instrument. You can place the books on a bookshelf, or you can install shelves on the walls to house them. You can also place head phones on the shelves along with the CDs. Their instruments can also be mounted on the wall by using shelves. Keep the music stands on the floor under the shelving.

Clothes

Sort

To thoroughly sort the clothing, you will need to pull every piece out of the drawers and off the hangers. You would then separate them into two piles. The first group will contain things that they no longer wear or that they have outgrown. If they have any items that are tattered and/or torn, then you should throw them out. The second group will be made up of the things that they still adorn themselves with.

Neaten

Clothes that they no longer wear or have outgrown, but are in relatively good condition, you can donate or sell. If there are things that they're not going to use within the next couple of months, you can store your extras. Place donations in the box marked "Donations". Place the things you're going to sell in the box labeled "Sale". Place the things you're going to store in the box marked "Storage". Put the things you're going to get rid of in the trash bag, and put your recyclables in another bag. Now, you have to tackle the things that they still use. Start by categorizing the remaining items. You will most likely have a huge pile of clothes on the floor, and you may need to sort the piles into clean and unclean. If unclean, then put it in the hamper.

Assign

The next task at hand is to seperate the remaining clean clothes into two piles: clothes they wear outside the house, and clothes that they wear around the house (for example: pajamas). So, you will end up with a pile of:

T-shirts (subdivide into house clothes and outside wear)

Pajamas

Robes

Shirts (sub-divide formal and casual)

Pants (subdivide into dressy and casual)

Dresses (subdivide into formal and casual)

Skirts (sub-divide into dressy and casual)

Jackets (subdivide these into dressy, suits jackets, and casual)

Sweaters (subdivide into dressy and casual)

Place

Now, you have to find a home for all of their clothes. You can start by figuring out what items are worn most often. If your kids wear pants and shirts most often, then these items should be put in a location that will enable your kids to have easy access to them; for example, in the front of the closet. If dresses are not worn regularly, then they should go to the back of the closet. You will then need to figure out what needs to be put in the drawers, and what should be hung in the closet. You can put clothes that are worn at home in drawers, and leave the closet available for things that are worn outside the home. Make sure that you don't overcrowd the drawers or closet. You may need additional storage for things. So, you may consider getting another dresser or sweater chest for your child's room. Remember, because of the large selection of storage items available to you in the stores, you can easily find something to blend in with the decor.

Socks and Underwear

Sort

You need to pull all of these items out of the drawers or off the floor, and closely examine them. Put them into piles of things that should be kept, and things that you can throw out.

Neaten

If the items that you no longer want are in relatively good condition, you can donate or sell them. If you have too many things that you're not going to use within the next couple of months, you can store your extras. Place donations in the box marked "Donations". Place the things you're going to sell in the box labeled "Sale". Place the things you're going to store in the box marked "Storage". Put the things you're going to get rid of in the trash bag, and put your recyclables in another bag.

Assign

The remaining items can then be categorized. Put them into piles of like items, such as:

Socks (subdivide into dressy and casual)

Pantyhose

Bras (subdivide into sporty and regular)

Underwear (subdivide into panties, boxers, briefs, etc.)

Undershirts (subdivide into t-shirt and camisoles)

Place

These items should all be given their own drawers. If you have big drawers and want to place a few of these items in the same drawer, you may need to buy containers that fit easily into the drawer to separate the items. For example, if you're going to place socks and bras in one drawer, you may need to buy two bins that fit into the drawer; one for the socks and one for the bras.

Coats and Outer Wear Accessories

Sort

Over time, one tends to accumulate a lot of clothes and accessories. Scarf sets seem to have increased in popularity of the past few years, and as a result, your child may have ended up with quite a few of them. First of all, you need to take inventory of all of the coats and accessories. Put them in a pile, and then divide them into two piles. The first pile will consist of things that are old, ripped, outdated, or don't fit any more. The second pile will contain the things that your child still wears and wants.

Neaten

If the items that you no longer want are in relatively good condition, you can donate or sell them. If they have too many things that they're not going to use within the next couple of months, you can store your extras. Place donations in the box marked "Donations". Place the things you're going to sell in the box labeled "Sale". Place the things you're going to store in the box marked "Storage". Put the things you're going to get rid of in the trash bag, and put your recyclables in another bag.

Assign

The items that your child still wants will need to be categorized. Most people just push their coats into the closet and leave it at that. However, it's a lot more effective if the coats were categorized by season and usage. You can start by categorizing them into winter, fall, spring, and summer. Once you have them in these piles, you can then further categorize them into dressy and casual. Remember to also categorize the outer wear accessories, like their hats, scarves, gloves, and umbrellas. Once you have these in different piles, you can place them with their corresponding coats. Therefore, you will put the winter accessories with the winter coats, the spring accessories, like umbrellas, with the spring coats, and so on.

Place

You can put the coats that are out of season in the back of the closet. The accessories that correspond with them can be placed on the shelf above them in the closet. You can buy a basket or container to place them in. If you buy stackable containers, you can label them. For example, winter accessories, spring accessories, etc.

Ties, Belts, Scarves, Hats, and Handkerchiefs
Sort

You know that your kids have a bunch of accessories, and sometimes it can be said that they have too many. Oh well, we just have to find a way to accommodate them. So, gather them all together in to a central location.

Neaten

If the items that you no longer want are in relatively good condition, you can donate or sell them. If they have too many things that they're not going to use within the next couple of months, you can store your extras. Place donations in the box marked "Donations". Place the things you're going to sell in the box labeled "Sale". Place the things you're going to store in the box marked "Storage". Put the things you're going to get rid of in the trash bag, and put your recyclables in another bag.

Assign

You can then further separate them in to their designated piles of ties, belts (subdivide into dressy and casual), hats (subdivide into dressy, casual, sporty, and fun), and scarves.

Place

You can place the ties in a tie organizer. That way, you will be able to view them at a glance. You can then place the tie organizer in the closet near to the dress shirts. The scarves can get hung on an accessory hanger, which can be placed near to the shirts and jackets. The belts can be put on an accessory hanger, as well. These can go in the closet near to the pants. The dressy hats can be kept on the shelf in the closet in Hat boxes. The sporty hats can be stacked on top of each other in a neat pile.

Shoes
Sort
Gather all the shoes from every corner of the room, and put them in a central location.

Neaten
If the items that you no longer want are in relatively good condition, you could donate or sell them. If they have too many things that they're not going to use within the next couple of months, you can store the extras. Place donations in the box marked "Donations". Place the things you're going to sell in the box labeled "Sale". Place the things you're going to store in the box marked "Storage". Put the things you're going to get rid of in the trash bag, and put your recyclables in another bag.

Assign
The shoes that are left will definitely need to be sub-divide into piles of dressy and casual.

Place
You may need to invest in a shoe organizer of some sort. There are so many on the market now. You can buy a shoe organizer that can be hung behind the door, a shoe rack, or some other shoe-holding device. Remember to keep them in their designated categories.

Jewelry, Sunglasses, Bags, and Hair Accessories
Sort
Collect all of their jewelry, sunglasses, bags, and hair accessories together.

Neaten

If the items that you no longer want are in relatively good condition, you can donate or sell them. If you have too many things that you're not going to use within the next couple of months, you can store your extras. Place donations in the box marked "Donations". Place the things you're going to sell in the box labeled "Sale". Place the things you're going to store in the box marked "Storage". Put the things you're going to get rid of in the trash bag, and put your recyclables in another bag.

Assign

You will have to put these items into several smaller piles, as well. So, you will end up with small piles of hair accessories (subdivide these into hair ties, hair pins and hair clips), jewelry (subdivide into costume jewelry and precious stones, gold, etc.), purses (subdivide into dressy and casual), bags (subdivide into school and other), and sunglasses.

Place

Find an appropriate place for the hair accessories; you may have to invest in a storage bin of some sort. The sunglasses will also need a home. You may need to install some shelves in the bedroom to accommodate the sun glasses. Jewelry commands a place of its own. You may need to invest in jewelry boxes for these trinkets. You are going to need one for the precious stones, and one for the costume jewelry. You may need additional space for these treasure chests. You can once again install some shelves for them. The purses and bags will also need a place to hang. You may want to install some wall hooks to accommodate them.

Hair Accessories
Sort

Gather all of the hair accessories, such as curling irons, blow dryers, steam curlers, flat irons, etc., into a central location. Comb through this mountain and create two piles. One will contain the items that are broken, or that your child no longer uses. The other will consist of the things that your child still wants and uses.

Neaten

If the items that you no longer want are in relatively good condition, you can donate or sell them. If you have too many things that you're not going to use within the next couple of months, you can store your extras. Place donations in the box marked "Donations". Place the things you're going to sell in the box labeled "Sale". Place the things you're going to store in the box marked "Storage". Put the things you're going to get rid of in the trash bag, and put your recyclables in another bag.

Assign

Hair accessories, such as curling irons, blow dryers, steam curlers, flat irons, etc., need to be grouped together into their own piles.

Place

You will definitely need a storage container for these. You can store these on a shelf in the closet. If you run out of space at any time, you can invest in a book shelf, or install some shelves for the accessories.

SNAP the Boxes

Now, it's time to SNAP the bags and boxes.

Sort

Place all the packed bags together, and place all the packed boxes together.

Neaten

Put all the Storage boxes together, all the Donation boxes together, and all the Sale boxes together. Now, group all the trash bags together, and all the bags with recyclables together.

Assign and Place

You can put all the trash bags in the garbage can and the recyclables in the recycle bin.

Place the Sale boxes in the garage, or designate an area that is out of the way. Make sure that you can easily access them when you're ready to have your sale.

You can load the Donation boxes in your car, so you can drive them to the thrift store. If you've rented a storage unit, you can place the Storage boxes in the car, and drive them to the storage unit, as well. If you plan on storing them at home, make sure they are out of the way and neatly stacked.

Reward

Now that you have made this room fit for the potential buyer to love, have some ice cream.

Scent

You can place a plug-in air freshener in the kids' rooms to ensure that it smells nice for your random spot checks!

Tip

Assign a color for each child. For example, your baby girl can have pink and your baby boy can have blue. Then, reinforce it by buying them pink and blue toothbrushes. You can buy them pink and blue toy chests, and put pink and blue knobs on their dresser drawers. You can also assign them a color coded-hamper.

Make sure that the kids can reach their clothes in the closet. You may need to lower the level of the bar in the closet. This will allow them to access their clothes, as well as replace them.

Maintenance

Make sure your kids go through their drawers every three months, and throw away torn or tattered clothing, as well as pull out items that they've outgrown.

Online Resource

Visit www.organizetosell.com for helpful tips and advice. You can also sign up for giveaways and contests too. This site was built with you in mind, so feel free to email your questions.

Joy Rich, LL.B.

Box List

Room Name:

Box #	Description of Contents

Notes:

Office: Before Picture

Office: After Picture

Chapter 9
Office

Home offices are a must have for most buyers. A lot of people work from home, or conduct business from home. They need an organized, calm place to work. By utilizing four simple steps (SNAP), you can breathe new life into this space. You just need to sort, neaten, assign, and place your things.

SNAP the Office

Before you begin organizing a room, make sure you have everything you need.

Here's a check list of everything you'll need:

1. A marker
2. A pen
3. Packaging tape
4. Scissors
5. A box for Donations
6. A box for Sale items
7. A box for Storage items
8. A garbage bag
9. A bag for recyclables
10. This book
11. Extra boxes and bags

Once a box is full, you should:

1. Tape it closed.
2. Assign it a number.
3. Write the room's name on it (for example: kitchen).
4. Write a short description of its contents on it (for example: dishes).
5. Fill out the Box List at the end of each chapter when you've completed the room. This will allow you to keep track of all your boxes in one place. As well, because the list is in the book, you won't misplace it!

At the end of each chapter, there is a "Notes" section. You can use this for any notes you may need to make while packing, or for things you will need to do while unpacking. Make sure to take an after picture, and place it at the beginning of the chapter below the before picture. The after picture will set a standard for you to maintain.

Papers, Bills, Letters, Cards, etc.
Sort
Gather up all the papers that you have all over the office. Put them in a central location.

Neaten
Go through the piles of papers, bills, letters, and cards, and then shred everything that you don't need.

Assign
Now, place these items into like piles. For example, you will end up with piles of phone bills, electricity bills, letters from friends, cards for every occasion, reports, memos, travel brochures, etc.

Place
You will need to invest in a filing system, if you don't already have one. You can buy a standard filing cabinet, or there are nifty wicker baskets that you

can purchase and use as a filing system. You need to place these items in a convenient way, so that they can be found. I suggest you designate a file drawer for the household. That way, you open up files for each bill, such as your insurance policies, utility bills, internet bills, etc., and house them in this drawer. I suggest you alphabetize all the files, so that they are easily accessible.

The letters and cards that you have received for every occasion imaginable could be placed in a keepsake box. You could buy one from the store, or you could make one. All you need is a shoe box, gift paper, and tape or glue. You can decorate it any way you want. Make sure you label it as well, so you know what is in it. You could put the year on it as well, so this way, you can store it chronologically. You can then place it on your bookshelf. If you don't have one, you can buy one or just install some shelves on the wall.

For your papers that you have decided to keep, you can start by opening up files for each item. So, you may have a file for contracts, memos, speeches, etc. Then, place them in the filing cabinet or filing system. In and out trays are great for items that you are currently working on. You can place all the items that you have received, such as mail, in your "In" tray, and items that you have completed in your "Out" tray (like assignments). You can also have a "Need To Be Filed" tray for all the items that you have to file away.

Books, Magazines, and Newspapers
Sort
Group all of your books, magazines, and newspapers into a central location.

Neaten
If the items that you no longer want are in relatively good condition, you can donate or sell them. If you have too many things that you're not going to use within the next couple of months, you can store your extras. Place donations

in the box marked "Donations". Place the things you're going to sell in the box labeled "Sale". Place the things you're going to store in the box marked "Storage". Put the things you're going to get rid of in the trash bag, and put your recyclables in another bag.

Assign

You can then categorize the remaining items into like stacks. For example:
Magazines (subdivide into sports, fitness, fashion, financial, etc.)
Newspapers
Books (subdivide into fiction, non-fiction, self-help, business, etc.)

Place

You will have to invest in a bookshelf and shelving to organize these items. For your magazines, I suggest that you designate a shelf or two for these items. Place them on the shelf in their respected groups. Your books, as well, should be placed on the shelves according to their respected categories. For example, the fiction books will get their own shelf, and so will the self-help books.

The newspapers need to be dealt with now. I suggest that you cut out the relevant sections in the newspaper that you want to keep, and recycle the rest of the paper. You can then place the cuttings in a scrap book. This way, you will be able to find the clippings easily. Scrap booking is also a way to relax and express yourself creatively.

Staplers, Rulers, Pens, Pencils, Letter Organizers, etc.
Sort

You can start by collecting these knick-knacks in a central location.

Neaten

If the items that you no longer want are in relatively good condition, you can donate or sell them. If you have too many things that you're not going to use within the next couple of months, you can store your extras. Place donations in the box marked "Donations". Place the things you're going to sell in the box labeled "Sale". Place the things you're going to store in the box marked "Storage". Put the things you're going to get rid of in the trash bag, and put your recyclables in another bag.

Assign

Place the remaining items into like groups. You should end up with something like this: stacks of pens, pencils, rulers, letter openers, etc.

Place

You now need to house these items in a convenient, but out of the way, location. I suggest keeping a lot of these items off of your desk. You should put your pens, pencils, rulers, letter openers, and staplers in your desk drawer. You can buy a few small containers to hold these items. Containers will separate these items, and make it easier for you to locate them.

Bags, Briefcases, Back Packs, etc.
Sort

You need to pull these out of their hiding places.

Neaten

If the items that you no longer want are in relatively good condition, you can donate or sell them. If you have too many things that you're not going to use within the next couple of months, you can store your extras. Place donations in the box marked "Donations". Place the things you're going to sell in the box labeled "Sale". Place the things you're going to store in the box marked "Storage". Put the things you're going to get rid of in the trash bag, and put your recyclables in another bag.

Assign

The bags that are remaining need to be categorized into like bags. You will have a group of brief cases, back packs, etc.

Place

These bags can be placed on a shelf of some kind. It could be the last shelf on your book shelf. You can even install some hooks on the wall and hang them, if you like. If you have a closet in the room, then you can use a shelf in there to house them.

Calculators, Computers, and Printers
Sort

You need to put all of these items on top of your desk, so that you can inspect them.

Neaten

If the items that you no longer want are in relatively good condition, you can donate or sell them. If you have too many things that you're not going to use within the next couple of month, you can store your extras. Place donations in the box marked "Donations". Place the things you're going to sell in the box labeled "Sale". Place the things you're going to store in the box marked "Storage". Put the things you're going to get rid of in the trash bag, and put your recyclables in another bag.

Assign

Put all you calculators together, and all of your computer accessories together.

Place

It is vital that you have enough room on your desk for your computer, as well as for you to work effectively. Therefore, you may need to get a larger desk, or expand the current work space that you have. Your printer does not have to be on your desk. It can go somewhere else. Your phone should be at your fingertips when you are at your desk, so put it in a convenient location. If the cord can't reach, then buy a longer chord! Your calculator should also be kept in a drawer and off the desk.

SNAP the Boxes

Now, it's time to SNAP the bags and boxes.

Sort

Place all the packed bags together, and place all the packed boxes together.

Neaten

Put all the Storage boxes together, all the Donation boxes together, and all the Sale boxes together. Now, group all the trash bags together, and all the bags with recyclables together.

Assign and Place

You can put all the trash bags in the garbage can and the recyclables in the recycle bin.

Place the Sale boxes in the garage, or designate an area that is out of the way. Make sure that you can easily access them when you're ready to have your sale. You can load the Donation boxes in your car, so you can drive them to the thrift store. If you've rented a storage unit, you can place the Storage boxes in the car, and drive them to the storage unit, as well. If you plan on storing them at home, make sure they are out of the way and neatly stacked.

Reward

Now that you have completed this project, give yourself a promotion from confused to enthused, and treat yourself. Schedule a massage for yourself at the spa!

Scent

Flowering plants are a great touch, because along with adding a touch of greenery, they add a nice fragrance.

Maintenance

Remember, consistency is key. Make sure that you place everything in its home when you're finished with it. If you do this every time you use something, then your office will remain clean and livable.

Online Resource

Visit www.organizetosell.com for helpful tips and advice. You can also sign up for giveaways and contests too. This site was built with you in mind, so feel free to email your questions.

Box List

Room Name:

Box #	Description of Contents

Joy Rich, LL.B.

Notes:

Notes:

Joy Rich, LL.B.

Attic and Basement: Before Picture

Attic and Basement: After Picture

Chapter 10
Attics and Basements

The basement and attic are two problem areas, because people pack them full of things and forget about them. Buyers want to see the potential in these spaces. They may want to convert them into living spaces, so this will require the spaces to be clean and clutter free. You just have to sort, neaten, assign, and place your things.

SNAP the Attic and Basement

Before you start, take a picture of the room. The before picture will allow you to see what you don't want the room to look like again. There's a blank page at the beginning of the chapter for before and after pictures. Before you begin organizing a room, make sure you have everything you need. Here's a check list of everything you'll need:

1. A marker
2. A pen
3. Packaging tape
4. Scissors
5. A box for Donations
6. A box for Sale items
7. A box for Storage items
8. A garbage bag
9. A bag for recyclables

10. This book

11. Extra boxes and bags

Once a box is full, you should:

1. Tape it closed.

2. Assign it a number.

3. Write the room's name on it (for example: kitchen).

4. Write a short description of its contents on it (for example: dishes).

5. Fill out the Box List at the end of each chapter when you've completed the room. This will allow you to keep track of all your boxes in one place. As well, because the list is in the book, you won't misplace it!

At the end of each chapter is a "Notes" section. You can use this for any notes you may need to make while packing, or for things you will need to do while unpacking. Make sure to take an after picture and place it at the beginning of the chapter below the before picture. The after picture will set a standard for you to maintain.

Sort

Don't store junk! Only store items that have sentimental or financial value. However, if you have a lot of things stored already, you can start by sorting your items. Bring your items into a pile. Designate everything into two piles. The first pile will consist of things that are broken, items that have no value or meaning to you, and things that you no longer want to hold on to. The second pile will consist of things that you want to keep.

Neaten

Throw out, recycle, donate, or sell items that have no value or meaning to you, as well as broken items. Chances are, if the items have been broken for a while, you're not going to fix it; so let it go! Now, all you have to do is box up the items in their respective boxes, and bag the trash and recyclables. If you have items that you will keep, you can place them in storage, so put them in the "Storage" box. If the items that you no longer want are in relatively good condition, you can donate or sell them. Place donations in the box marked "Donations". Place the things you're going to sell in the box labeled "Sale".

Assign

Categorize the remaining items that are left. You can put them into piles of similar objects. For example: pictures, books, lamps, collectables, etc.

Place

You may need to buy boxes, bins, shelves, and bookshelves to store your items.

You can color-code the bins and boxes. For example, you can use green for items of value, and yellow for sentimental items. You can also display items that you have collected on shelves. Another helpful hint is for you to place your books and albums on bookshelves, that way, you can access them easily.

Tip

Make a picture file of your boxes. It's easy. All you have to do is take a picture of the inside of the box before you close it. That way, you can download it to your computer and know exactly what's in each box. If you have a lot of boxes that look alike, number them on the inside and outside. So, if it's the first box; write 1 on the inside so you can see it in the picture, and then write 1 on the outside, so you can see it when it's closed. Then, when you save the picture on your computer, you can name it Box 1. You may also want to paint the walls with a vibrant color to brighten up the space.

SNAP the Boxes

Now, it's time to SNAP the bags and boxes.

Sort

Put all the packed bags together, and put all the packed boxes together.

Neaten

Put all the Storage boxes together, all the Donation boxes together, and all the Sale boxes together. Now, group all the trash bags together, and all the bags with recyclables together.

Assign and Place

You can put all the trash bags in the garbage can and the recyclables in the recycle bin.

Place the Sale boxes in the garage, or designate an area that is out of the way. Make sure that you can easily access them when you're ready to have your sale. You can load the Donation boxes in your car, so you can drive them to the thrift store. If you've rented a storage unit, you can place the Storage boxes in the car, and drive them to the storage unit, as well. If you plan on storing them at home, make sure they are out of the way and neatly stacked.

Reward

Now that you've finally organized this space, make sure you do something nice for yourself, you've earned it. It can be something as simple as taking some time out to listen to your old CDs, or just spending some time browsing through those old photo albums.

Scent

You should purchase and install an automatic air freshener. These are great for basements, because they will automatically dispense a puff of fragrance periodically, so you don't have to. This will keep the basement or attic smelling great!

Maintenance

When you want to store new items in the attic or basement, make sure that they're placed in the location designated for them. For example, if you're going to be storing another album, then place it on the bookshelf with the others. If you are going to be storing a new item in the basement or attic, then make sure that you designate a home for it. As well, make sure that you make new photo files for any additional boxes that you may store.

Online Resource

Visit www.organizetosell.com for helpful tips and advice. You can also sign up for giveaways and contests too. This site was built with you in mind, so feel free to email your questions.

Box List

Room Name:

Box #	Description of Contents

Notes:

Joy Rich, LL.B.

Notes:

Chapter 11
Celebrate

Congratulations! You now live in an organized house! This is a momentous occasion that needs to be marked with a celebration! For this grandiose event, you may want to invite some friends, family, or neighbors over to show off your new surroundings. This shin dig will reinforce the fact that your home looks fantastic, because you will be flooded with complements by your guests. This get-together will also give you something to live up to. Your home is now ready to be seen by potential buyers! By organizing your space, you can command top dollar for it.

Consistency is the key to maintaining an organized home. You should also keep in mind that everything has a home. So, make sure that it resides there everyday!

Remember, if you ever have to deal with an unorganized area, make sure you use the **SNAP** method to tidy it up. By simply sorting, neatening, assigning, and placing, you can organize your way out of any mess!

Visit www.organizetosell.com for helpful tips and advice. You can also sign up for giveaways and contests too. This site was built with you in mind, so feel free to email your questions.

Box List

Room Name:

Box #	Description of Contents

Box List

Room Name:

Box #	Description of Contents

Joy Rich, LL.B.

Box List

Room Name:

Box #	Description of Contents

Box List

Room Name:

Box #	Description of Contents

Joy Rich, LL.B.

Notes:

Notes: